The Armenian Identity Examined: What is He?

Michael Boyajian

Jera Studios Publishing

The Armenian Identity Examined: What is He?

Michael Boyajian

ISBN: 9781795799157

Jera Studios Publishing

I dedicate this book to my wife Jeri

whose idea this was and to the bully

who became my friend, Paul S.

Contents

Author's Note

This idea that you stop a bully by
pushing back a bully is an urban myth.
You stop a bully by enduring a bully until
the bully becomes your friend. This
then becomes part of your identity.

Michael Boyajian, February 2019

Introduction

What does it mean to be Armenian?

There are many approaches to identity. One is psychological, it is how you identify yourself. Another is sociological which is how you define your identity in society. Anthropologically speaking identity is about differences and how we set ourselves apart.

A crisis in identity can have an adverse impact on the individual or group. Knowing one's identity and place in society can increase self-esteem and reduce depression and anxiety.

Through my personal experiences, travels and study I will examine identity as it specifically applies to Armenians in the homeland or as part of the global diaspora, and the changes of identity that exist from diaspora nation to diaspora nation. I will also explore to the impact of the genocide, the post genocide, the Republic, the Second Republic on how Armenians define themselves.

It is important to remember that the identity of the Armenians in the homeland and the diaspora are not static, but fluid and ever changing in response to the environment in which they reside. The diaspora, as it always has, changes with levels of oppression, economy and opportunity. As history has shown, Armenians will not stay in an area to simply maintain an Armenian presence but will migrate to a place free of oppression with better opportunities. They will establish a diaspora in an environment where they can thrive, which has been the case since Julfa and India and the Genocide.

How someone defines themselves within the diaspora varies from region to region even within the same nation. Generational differences, and the level of integration within the larger community are also key factors in identity. Additionally, how does someone's proximity to the genocide affect their identity? What is the impact on identity of those that actually knew a genocide survivor as opposed to a young person who only knows of a survivor from stories told around the kitchen table?

Through my personal journey to fully discovering and embracing my identity as an Armenian I hope to address these questions.

 "All identities, whether religious, national, ethnic, political, or gender-based give members a sense of belonging, relatedness, and of safety within the group. " Kathryn Margules Sajdak, MSW.

 "Identity relates to our basic values that influence our choices, reflecting who we are. We internalize our identity from our parents and our culture." Anna M. Cognetto, LCSW-R.

Chapter 1

"Who are you? Who, who. Who, who. Who are you? " Pete Townsend, The Who.

It is the end of the last period of Third Grade class for today. The bell rings. I am the first one out the door running towards home chased by a pack of bullies. They catch me and throw me into a sticker bush. I do not know why they do this. Then they force me to fight Peter. Peter and I don't want to fight each other but they make us fight or else they will throw us into the sticker bush. We fight with punches

that hold back real anger and power.
They land harmlessly but only Peter and
I know that. The pack is satisfied.

I head to home where you cannot tell
your parents what is happening because
things will only make the situation
worse. You don't know why you're
being bullied, why any of this is
happening. They call me brillo head
because of my dark curly hair. I try to
straighten my hair but then they call me
"plateau head".

What you do know is that before you
moved to Long Island you were in
Kindergarten in Queens finger painting
with other students who were different

than one another but everyone was happy. Then your parents moved you to the suburbs in the middle of the school year and the bullying started.

In Third Grade a student in a coonskin hat asks you what religion are you? You think this is your big moment to make friends and explain your Christian faith. You answer what your mother had told you, Apostolic. The kid points his finger at you and screams he is an atheist. Ten kids jump on you and start punching you as the teacher looks on with disdain. You lay broken on the ground a son of the first Christian nation, 301 AD, decades before Rome. No one is told of this, your parents never know.

But when you push back by acting out by throwing giant spitballs called cannonballs around the class the principal calls your father at work in the city. When you go home you will be punished. Those that beat you up don't even remember beating you up.

You act out even more becoming a trouble maker with one of the bullies. They decide to separate you both in Fourth Grade. He stays in his track. You are sent down to Special Ed. Here you find other people who are different. A black student. A gay student. An Asian student. You are like the Island of Misfit Toys. You are all friends. It is happy.

You excel at your courses. The teacher
is a good teacher, she knows you don't
belong here. You are sent back to your
track with the warning that if you start
trouble again it is back to Special Ed.

You excel now. Now the bullies are mad
because you are smart. The teachers
like smart students and you are now
protected. The teachers don't like
students who are not smart. They beat
up this one student who cannot excel
thinking he is lazy. In the future people
will realize that he had a learning
disability and was not lazy.

They beat up another student. A short
kid who falls to his knees begging the

teacher not to hit him because he cannot say the Pledge because he cannot say the word God. He is a Jehovah Witness. They beat him for not saying God.

Then you make it to Junior High and the first year here is a bully fest but by the second year, Eighth Grade they are all gone. And there is peace and you become friends with the bully who was your comrade in Elementary School.

You organize a Jerry Lewis muscular dystrophy carnival. You have Hi C and cookies. You play games. You have puppet shows with a theater made out of a cardboard washing machine box

and the puppets are white tube socks
with lipstick where the mouth are. You
raise some money for Jerry Lewis and
the kids with MD but more importantly
you make everyone in the
neighborhood aware of their plight.
You now have compassion.

Now that you have compassion, you
begin to have awareness of your mind.
Courses interest you. The English
teacher introduces you to Catch 22 and
you learn to laugh reading it. The music
teachers introduce you to Tommy, Jesus
Christ Superstar and the moog
synthesizer. You paint abstract things in
art class. You make people laugh with
your silly stories read aloud. History
really interests you, American history.

Science and math are a wonder, there is a magic to the universe. You learn this from the Periodic Chart in Chemistry and Earth Science and Biology and the formulas of Algebra, Geometry and Trigonometry.

You are now in High School. There is no bullying here and you have good friends. You watch Karate movies and listen to fusion music. You also start seeing films at the Mini Cinema in Uniondale. The Woodstock movie, Rocky Horror, Underground movies, Jimi Hendrix.

But now dad loses his job. The technology of his skill, photoengraving,

has been replaced. Most
photoengravers are Armenians. He is a
World War II vet who saw his best
friend die on the runway in a plane
crash. His entire crew disappeared on a
flight he did not go on. You and your
dad used to go to Yankee Stadium, to
stadiums to see Joe Namath and the
Jets and the football Giants. You build
electronic kits together. You are
friends. He is a big man. And he snaps.
And he is angry and his anger is directed
at you. In the future this will be called
PTSD.

Your friends have the same problems.
One friend, a guitarist, shows you the
places he hides when his father comes
home. People must notice things. The

angry yelling. No one does anything.
You run out of the house but where can
you go. You go to the park. But then
you go home because there is nowhere
to go.

You think of joining the army. The
recruiter calls. You talk. It is a close
decision. But then you're off to college
and everyone is really nice here and the
professors like you and you become a
popular kid and you go home with self-
esteem. And your brother and sister are
happy now and your mom is happy, dad
is quiet but not angry. Grandma is
there, she doesn't speak English. We
can communicate with her even though
dad said not to teach us Armenian
because it would affect our learning.

But how did that affect him, he skipped grades when he was in school in the city. You don't care because you have self-esteem now.

Your mind becomes more aware as you excel at Astronomy, American History, American Literature, Native Americanism, Statistics, and Criminal Justice. Then you transfer to another school a better school and the troubles return. This time though they are subtle below the surface. The people running the school move the goal posts on you, some people take advantage of you. You begin to drink, you begin to flunk out. You have no money for food. You decide to drop out. You tell everyone you are going to be a writer.

23

On the last day at the school you see thugs come into the dorm and start smashing furniture. The RA tries to stop them but they beat him up, you go to help and they beat you up. You go home with a black eye and no future, your mom looks at you like it is your fault. You must pay a small monthly rent to your mom and get a job.

You end up in a mailroom. You excel here. The corporation likes you and you get raises and there is talk of how you might become an executive. You become friends with your boss who is older than you but you learn you have something in common with him. The universal language of sports. You are both Yankees fans. He takes you under his wing. You will be there even when you go back to college and until he retires. He is good.

You make a decision after not being published for a year. You will go back to that school and this time succeed. You go back and this time you excel. History of New York, History of South Africa, Chinese Intellectual History, Modern Literature, James Joyce, Fiction Writing.

You are told in order to graduate you must now take a foreign language. You wonder if they are moving the goal posts. But this time they help you and say there is an exception. You can take courses that are English translations of foreign language literature. You are amazed by these authors. It is a new world.

Then they say you cannot graduate and again you think the goal posts are moving but then you say can I see the bill. And you see your name on the bill but this person has a different middle initial than you. You tell the administrator this. They check the social security numbers and realize it is not you. You can graduate next year.

Chapter 2

One day your friend brings a gift to your home on your birthday. It is your future wife, Jeri. You go on a date but nothing happens. The last semester you meet on the Stony Brook train and love happens. She is an artist and you are a writer. You are in a new world and all is happy again and you are both ready to graduate and start your careers and what will be your life together.

You begin a career in publishing. First books than magazines. You move to Brooklyn to go to law school and you learn African Americans are not what are portrayed on TV. You also learn that what is portrayed on TV is not reality and that there is nothing wrong with being Armenian, or Armenian food or the Armenian Church. Now the bullies are saying you are the bully...

Ok so that is the beginnings of my identity as an Armenian. So now the question is what binds all of us together as Armenians? The church, culture, food, the homeland, family, language, ethnicity, history or perhaps the genocide itself. The church in Bayside Queens bound many Armenians together who were dispersed across

Long Island and the outer boroughs.
Every Sunday Holy Martyr's Church was
like a beacon drawing in a full crowd of
Armenians.

In India all that really remains of the
Armenians are the churches. And these
churches still stand and take in visitors
curious about the Armenians. The
church is so important that when I was
young families would have the priest
over for dinner once every few months
on a regular basis.

The Armenian community builds a
magnificent cathedral on Second
Avenue in Manhattan, St. Vartan's. In
Julfa the churches are in pristine

condition and operating at capacity.
They are, like the India churches, great
works of architecture that have fused
the local accents with the Armenian
style. For some reason the churches in
America go by the Armenian style alone.

When I was kid and being bullied the
church gave me a glow in the dark cross
that I would keep by my bedside. I
would fall asleep with it glowing
peacefully in the dark. Churches are so
important to Armenians that you are
likely to find an Armenian church
wherever you are visiting before you
would even find an Armenian
restaurant.

Let's look at wealth. Generally speaking the Armenians have some degree of wealth and this can be seen in their capacity to support the building and membership of churches and cathedrals. Much of this money is funneled to the educational institutions by groups like the AGBU and the Gulbenkian Foundation. This author went through law school with a Gulbenkian scholarship.

Unfortunately unlike the Catholics, there is no vast network of schools or even hospitals but for those of a few countries outside the United States. Of course there are Sunday schools at the churches.

When Armenians gather at churches for religious events or for weddings, food dance and music are an important part of the religious celebration.

Another important part of the church is its ability to draw together all Armenians. Even young people who are not a hundred percent Armenian take an interest in this part of their heritage. They ask the question as does this book, What am I?

Looking at the food aspect, it is a mix of Greek, Turkish and Persian accents. You can speculate that this unity of cuisines goes back at least to Byzantium or it

might just be a common east
Mediterranean basin style of cuisine.

Millions of dollars poured into Armenian
from the diaspora after the devastating
earthquake there decades ago at the
end of the Soviet period. This money
was a lifeline that the collapsing Soviet
Empire could not provide.   The dream
of a homeland was that close to being
snuffed out by the large losses of life
and property. And that is another thing
that binds us, our homeland, Armenia
with Mt. Ararat in the distance.

There is always talk of visiting Armenia
from wherever you may be in the
diaspora. You may not end up going but

you are compelled to want to go though some magnetic attraction not unlike the hypnotic draw of the pyramids of Egypt on most of the world's people or Mecca for Muslims.

Then there is the long two part linguistics story. First there is the spoken language that goes back centuries before the birth of Christ. Then there is the written language developed in 401 AD. Those who speak Armenian are looked up to as better Armenians although I have been told that what is important is that you are helping out. But our intellectuals insist that if you want to be an Armenian classicist than you better speak Armenian before Latin or Greek.

This is funny because the written language did not develop until the near end of antiquity in 401 AD. The oldest examples of the written language are bibles not scrolls of Plato and Aristotle. So the written language is squarely in the Christian era not even in the pagan epoch.

Again the church pops up. Hardly anything other than the Garni Temple exists from the Hellenistic/Roman period.   And even with that certain intellectuals are claiming that this obvious Roman temple is actually part of a Christian monastic complex.

You could see this this in the recent Armenia! exhibition at the Metropolitan Museum of Art. The show opens up with a khachkar, an Armenian Christian burial marker. Inside the show you find a map of churches in the Ottoman Empire and lots of bibles. So I argue that the Church and its symbols are a major thing that binds us together.

Is there something else that unites us greatly today? What topic will fill New York's Times Square, the crossroads of the world, with a million people every April? The Armenian Genocide, the cataclysm that wiped our three fourths of Armenians – 1.5 million were wiped out to be exact. After that we were hanging on by a thread saved only by the intellectual powerhouse of Paris which helped Armenians to rebuild their cultural institutions.

It can be argued that the genocide, meant to destroy us, has made us stronger in our unity. It draws together many Armenians of diverse backgrounds. The genocide is a lighthouse for wayward Armenians drawing them back into the flock. And is the denial of the genocide frustrating? Yes, but those who argue denial look like fools.   Like my dad used to say, if it did not happen than where are all my uncles? We have to convince modern Turks that we are not blaming them for what happened but the Ottomans urged on by the Kaiser.

The Ottomans first came for the professionals, teachers and doctors. There was a knock at the door, you were taken away and you were never seen again. After that they went after the rural peasants in the interior. Men, women and children were raped, marched into the desert to die and killed if they fell.

Ambassador Morgenthau suspects that the senile Turkish sultan was manipulated by the Kaiser. Some even say it was a fatwah. The atrocities were widely reported to no avail. Even Ernest Hemmingway writing for the Toronto Star could not save the day. The slaughter happened before and after 1915 and was not limited to Armenians but included Greeks and other Christian minorities. The screaming from the quays of Smyrna each night were Greeks and Armenians being killed.

And this Greek and Armenian kinship goes back to Alexander the Great and even earlier to Herodotus and Xenophon. When I went to Greece I was treated like royalty to the point that my wife looked at one flight attendant and said actually he is Armenian and not Greek. And the attendant laughed and said, same thing, same thing.

And today after our rebirth in Paris following the genocide there is a virtual Renaissance of Armenian art, music and literature. And in 2019 the Nubar Library has put out a call for papers discussing Armenian language newspapers. This has caused a groundswell of support for Armenians and their arts and culture.

Let's look at the history of Armenians now. Growing up we didn't know of Armenian heroes but they existed on the scale of the greatest of Greeks, Romans and Persians. Here are their stories.

Tigranes the Great is where the story of Armenia's heroic age should begin but our history goes back further to the times of Darius, Herodotus, Xenophon, Alexander and before that the proto Armenians who we know of from 6,000 year old wine making archaeological discoveries in a cave in Armenia.

We begin though with the Persians whose literature first mentions the Armenians years before the Histories of Herodotus. At this times the Armenians seem to be semi-independent from Persia. We know this because the primary sources report that they were allowed to keep their weapons. We can also surmise this because of the Persian custom of demanding subservience.

And that was to ask the target people for a handful of their soil as a symbol of their surrender without need of conflict. Many peoples opted for this and were allowed to remain in control of their kingdoms merely paying tribute.

The Persians tried this with the Greeks. The Greeks laughed at the diplomats and killed them and threw them into a pit to be eaten by dogs. This did not go over well with the Persians and conflict became inevitable.

The Persians assembled the greatest army ever seen and marched on Greece. At one point while crossing a waterway the Persian king ordered his soldiers to spear the water in order to kill it. Anyhow they arrived and at Marathon they were defeated by a greatly outnumbered Athenian force.

This is where the name for the running event comes from, marathon. A runner was deployed before the battle to Sparta to ask for help. The runner made the run of 20 some odd miles relayed the message, the Spartans said no and he died.

Well there was a little more to the story than that. The Spartans were a very religious society and they were in the middle of one of their holidays. They did send troops. 300 under Leonidas to Thermopylae to halt the Persian advance into their region giving the Athenians time to deploy their navy. They held the pass but were betrayed and slaughtered by the Persians but for Spartans this was a good way to die. And they did delay the Persians. The Athenians maneuvered their fleet into the narrow straits of Salamis and drew in the Persian navy as their king watched from the shoreline. Because the Persians were squeezed in they lost their numerical advantage and were wiped out by the Greeks. The king who was watching from shore thought it wise now to hurry back to Persia.

A few notes, first when your plane lands in Athens today from the United States you fly over Salamis. Secondly when you are atop the Acropolis standing in front of the Parthenon looking out the entranceway to the holy site you will see Salamis in the distance. This was no coincidence but the intent of Pericles who ruled over the rebuilding of the Acropolis. The original had been burned to the ground by the Persians.

After Salamis, the Greeks think that they are free of the Persians but the Persians manipulate Sparta and Athens into a war that would last a generation. This war so weakened Sparta and Athens that the forces of Phillip of Macedonia and his son Alexander were able to take control of Greece.

Alexander's father was assassinated. Alexander then became king and immediately began his invasion of Persia which would result in him conquering the known world.

How great was Alexander? Well as a little boy he watched as his father was horse trading. One large black horse was brought before him but it was too wild to be tamed and was refused by Phillip. But his son had been watching and he said to his father I will buy him and tame him. The father laughed but

thinking it a good time to teach the boy
a lesson agreed to the proposal.

What Alexander had noticed was that
the horse was not wild but afraid of his
shadow. He pointed the horse towards
the sun so that he could not see his
shadow and jumped up on him and
galloped him away and back to the
cheers of the Macedonians. The proud
father said to his son, you are going to
need a bigger kingdom than Macedonia.

Alexander the Great swept over Persia
but according to the Armenians never
conquered Armenia. The sources are
mixed on this and Alexander said he did
indeed conquer Armenia. But we think

both sides are correct. He may not have
gone to battle with them but they
agreed to serve under him. We can say
this because Armenian soldiers were
found as far away as India and the only
way they could have gotten there was
as part of Alexander's great army.

But enough of this, let's turn now to the
Romans. The Armenian king, Tigranes
the Great, built a great Hellenic Empire
complete with a capital city
Tigranocerta that was a major center for
Hellenism. It had all things Greek
including a theater at which Tigranes'
son wrote plays. Yes, the upper classes
supported all of this but the insular rural
Armenians stuck to their Eastern ways
and Parthian gods. But the system

worked nonetheless and there was much peace and prosperity. A Pax Armenia if you will.

Well the Romans referred to the Mediterranean as Nostrum Mare or Our Sea so if there was a rising power in the basin then it would raise eyebrows in the Roman senate. And the rise of Armenia did show up on the Roman radar.

Rome had been engaged elsewhere to begin with and that is one of the main reasons there was a power vacuum in the region that the Armenians filled with their great empire. Well responding to a threat real or perceived

as only Romans can an army was raised
and Lucullus was put in command by
the senate.

We can only speculate what first
contact was like between Rome and
Tigranes' Empire. The reputation of the
Romans had to have preceded their
arrival so there must have been some
trepidation. Yet Tigranes was a heroic
figure and met the challenge headfirst.

He and the Romans fought from one
end of Armenia to the other with cities
being taken and then retaken until after
ten years they found themselves where
they began at a standstill. Tigranes
must have assumed that like any enemy

ten years of war was quite enough. But
these were Romans and so rather than
retreat they merely changed
commanders.

Pompey the Great took command of the
Roman forces. And once again the
fighting resumed. This time though
Pompey gained the upper hand and
Tigranes came to the bargaining table.
Pompey said to him give me your
kingdom and you will have a friend for
life with Rome. Tigranes complied and
then Pompey gave him back his
kingdom with even more territory
requiring only tribute. He called
Tigranes the Great the King of Kings.

And so for the next 500 years Armenia would for the most part be a Roman client state and a buffer between Rome in the West and Parthia in the East. There would be some deviations like when the richest man in the world Crassus decided to invade Armenia for no real reason and he and his Roman standards were captured by the enemy and he was drowned in molten gold.

Then there was Antony and Cleopatra. An Armenian king was wary of fighting with Antony against Parthia finding Antony a bit of an idiot. So the Armenians kind of backed out of the fighting. This infuriated Antony and Cleopatra and Antony captured the Armenian king and his family and put

them in gold chains and sent them to
Cleopatra.

The couple were strapped for cash and
so tried to find out the location of the
Armenian crown jewels. The king did
not comply and Cleopatra executed the
king. On the urging of Antony's rival
Augustus the Roman Senate was
infuriated and condemned the action.
No one but the senate could execute a
client king. This tipped the balance to
Augustus and Antony and Cleopatra
went down to suicidal defeat. Augustus
took power and became the first among
equals and so begins the Pax Romana.

Centuries later Trajan would make
Armenia into a province but on his
death his successor Hadrian begged to
differ and returned Armenia to its
somewhat independent client state
status. And that's where it stood until
Constantine saw Christian symbols in
the sky and had his soldiers paint them
on their shields and went on to defeat
his rival at Milvian Bridge creating a
Christian oriented Roman Empire.

At around the same time in Armenia
Tiradates the Great makes Armenia the
first Christian nation in 301 AD decades
before Rome would make such a status
official. Tiradates and Constantine meet
and they must have talked to one
another about this thing called

Christianity and then the two peoples went their separate ways until, Byzantium.

Beginning with the Byzantine Empire Armenians become a manpower source. They are no longer a client state or a buffer. Still, the ranks of the Byzantines were filled with Armenian emperors, empresses, generals, artisans, religious leaders, intellectuals and soldiers.

Many of these Armenians became the greatest historical figures of their times in numbers too great to list in detail here. The Byzantines are actually Romans and describe themselves as such. The only differences being that the earlier Roman Empire was pagan and centered in the West. The Byzantines are Christians centered in the East. We are more familiar with the Western Romans because Edward Gibbons chose to downplay the attributes of the Eastern Romans.

Many people believe that the one thousand year decline of the Byzantines was historical fact. The truth is that the empire expanded and contracted over most of its history going into a steady decline only in its last century or two. During this time Armenia was overrun by a succession of powers ranging from Persians to Arabs to Ottomans. So Armenia was no longer a client state but again a source for manpower for Byzantium.

The Byzantines carried out great accomplishments in the arts, as can be seen in the numerous Byzantine exhibitions at the Metropolitan Museum of Art, and in the law, and military science with Greek Fire which was something like napalm and with architecture as can be seen in the Hagia Sophia. They missed the discovery of the New World by a just a few decades. What would their role have been in the New World? Certainly not a passive one.

The seeds of the global Armenia diaspora were planted at this time with many Armenians serving outside the homeland, with a new Armenian Kingdom operating out of Cilicia and with the traditional homeland being overrun by foreign powers as described above. But as the Buddhists say everything is impermanent. Eventually the mighty walls of the Byzantine capital, Constantinople, fell to the Ottomans and a new chapter opened up for the Armenians. It was a time of Ottoman oppression, liberation by a benevolent Persian shah and further migration to India.

When Shah Abbas of Persia attacked the Ottoman Empire the Armenians were a cohesive minority within the Ottoman Empire without a homeland. They were oppressed, persecuted and unappreciated yet they endured as many others have endured the bullying of the oppressor.

The Armenians caught the shah's attention. He had defeated the Ottomans but knew he could not hold his ground against them. So he decided on a scorched Earth retreat taking many of the ethnic minorities including the Armenians back to Persia. The Armenians were treated kindly by the Shah who liked them and they did better than the other groups during the long hard march into Persia to the capital Isfahan.

Upon their arrival in Isfahan the Shah built a magnificent city across the river and named it New Julfa after the city the Armenians had come from, Julfa. There were mansions and magnificent churches as well. Then the Armenians won the trading rights for silk in Persia and prosperity swept over them and Persia and the diaspora in general.

They built a worldwide trading network based on silk. The men would travel to the far outposts of the network while the woman stayed home and did the accounting, contract negotiations and drafting and much more. It was capitalism with a fundamental unit of the family at its base. The money poured into the Armenians who in turned poured it into the empire. They were the monetary fuel of the Persian Empire.

The Shah knew that if he treated the Armenians well they would stay but if they were treated poorly they would leave. The trading network stretched across the globe to Moscow and Britain into the Mediterranean and down to India and over to Australia and the Philippines.

Some say that New Julfans arrived at Jamestown in Virginia and saved that colony from failure by introducing modern agricultural concepts. This is in contradistinction to the fact that around this time slaves were being brought in and the economy there was changing into a plantation system of agriculture. There was one Armenian of note, Martin the Armenian, as well as a few others.

The Armenians in Persia respected the Muslim traditions there while keeping their Christian faith. Even their churches paid tribute to Muslim architecture while mainlining the Byzantine style. But then the shah died and his successors did not care much for the Armenians and oppression returned and the New Julfa trading empire was eaten up by the European powers. It was time to move again only this time the center of the diaspora shifted to India with trading rights in several coastal cities and a few inland as well.

Like the shah, the Mughal rulers of India liked the Armenians and saw much could be gained from them and so they were granted trading rights years before the European powers. Churches went up in a fusion fashion of Indian and Armenian motifs. Only this time more was traded than just silk, there were other commodities as well like textiles.

They did so well that the European powers approached them seeking help finding in roads to the Mughal rulers. The Armenians helped out not realizing they were undermining their own businesses. Britain benefited greatly from the Armenian help.   And when they took over India they remembered this and prosperity stayed with the Armenians.

But then with independence in the 20th Century the Armenians began to worry that the new Indian rulers were not fond of capitalism unlike today. They began to move again. This time to other places including Australia and New Zealand. Still a strong population remained in India.

Until that is the collapse of the Soviet Empire and the rise of the Armenian Republic, the free and independent homeland. Now the remaining Armenians in India migrated to the homeland and today only around a hundred Armenians remain in India but the churches still stand and thrive. This leads us to the new shape of the diaspora where there is an Armenian population in almost every country to the point that the diasporas are almost like multinational corporations crossing borders with ease and larger than the homeland.

It is a true miracle of survival when you think about the fact that 1.5 million Armenians were wiped out in the genocide, three fourths of all the Ottoman Armenians and yet thanks to Paris they were able to rebound and in the words of one of the Godfather movie characters, they are bigger than US Steel. Or better yet in today's world bigger than Apple Computing.

Chapter 3

One of the first things I noticed after moving from homogenous Long Island to Brooklyn was that I now blended with the local population. It was no longer What is he? But is he Latino, Jewish, Italian, Arabic, Asian, Greek, Serbian, Iranian, French, Spanish, Portuguese?

Yes a Latino thought I was a Latino and a Jew thought I was a Jew so on and so forth. Then you begin to question your Euro centric belief in Armenian geography and you look at a map and Armenia is in Asia and therefore you are Asian.

Then you study your ever changing DNA
results. But always you are 65 percent
Armenian but one day a large part
Jewish and then Southern European and
suddenly today 85 percent Armenian
and 15 Iranian. So maybe you were
from New Julfa sometime centuries ago.

When I was teaching ESL at Fordham my
students were from all over the world –
Asia, Europe, South America. Because
we all kind of blended the students had
an affinity for me and they helped me
knowing I had never really taught
before because I was a former judge not
a former teacher.

Let's just say they updated my tech skills from CDs and DVDs to Social Media. Because of this while the other teachers were using blackboards I was using audio visual techniques. For instance we would watch a movie with English subtitles. So they would be immersed in the language. Then we would write a paper on the movie in English and then read it aloud to the class in English. So my class excelled above all others.

Part of their day was spent touring New York and so I would either give them questions to answer on what they saw or they could write on their own about what they saw. Accents were the big topic. So many accents in New York. As for the questions, well they used Google to answer them but that is OK because now they knew the answer to the questions and who cares how they figured it out.

You cannot judge a book by its cover but blending can sure help. And I don't mean to discriminate but even if you don't blend you can dress to blend and that works just as well. Or you can act to blend like I did with my boss when I worked in a mailroom. My boss was a 60 year old Scotsman and I was a 20 year old punk rocker but we found common ground because we were both Yankee fans. You see sports are the universal language.

But what is it like to blend with other Armenians. Well you eat the same food, know the same religion, know the wedding dances and know basic Armenian phrases at the very least. And this food is readily available in other ethnic restaurants, Turkish, Arabic, Greek.

Ok that gives you an idea of what identity is or what we were calling blending is in the American Armenian diaspora but what about overseas? What is the diaspora like when you travel to Europe and run into Armenians from Europe and elsewhere? Let's discuss this layer of identity.

71

When I reached the top of the legal profession and became a judge my wife Jeri and I began traveling the world. I quickly learned that we Armenians blend, we do not stick out for the most part. It seems to be part of our post genocide identity. My uncle Gary A. Kulhanjian has a fear of being taken away by the Turks based on survivors telling him their stories when he was a child. Fly below the radar and they will not see you and come and take you away.

Also when I say the phrase, What is He? I do not use the male word He for male purposes but rather as a quote when Jeri and I first got married and we were apartment hunting and the landlords

would whisper to the real estate agent,
What is He? Is he Jewish? Does he
sleep with a cross over his bed?

And yet on my world travels I have
never heard anyone say, What is He?
You either knew I was American from
my style of dress or Armenian from
physical appearance or both. This was
proven in Paris when we were rescued
by an Armenian cab driver who
appeared out of nowhere during a
rainstorm and in Frankfurt when I
arrived at the airport injured and an
Armenian airport worker appeared and
had us carted to a special waiting area
and then to our gate.

During our first trip to London we did
not hear an English accent for three
days. So we were all blending you might
say. We were treated so well in the UK
that we returned four times and once
more to Edinburgh.

Then there was Florence which is a
capital of the Renaissance. And Rome
the eternal city where you will find a
statue of St. Gregory the Illuminator at
the Vatican. In these cities we were just
another ethnic couple from the states.

At the Alhambra in Spain we found the
very spot where Muslim, Christian and
Jew came together to create one of the
greatest works of beauty the world has

ever seen. They also saved civilization by translating many ancient texts. I was just another Spaniard here in their eyes.

One thing people in the places we visit do know once I start talking is that I am a New Yorker because of my New York accent. I was told in Athens that the way they know this is from all the old movies where every actor had a New York accent.

This is especially true of 1930s Hollywood productions but you can see it in 1950s monster movies where the scientists, victims, soldiers, press, heroes, good guys and bad guys all had

New York accents even the visitor from outer space had a New York accent.

In Key Largo lead Chicago bad guy Johnny Rocco has a New York accent as does good guy Humphrey Bogart and Lauren Bacall and the deputies and the Seminole Indians and everyone in Key Largo for that matter.

Even the movie Jaws has a New York accent cast from the chief to the scientist to the mayor and on and on in this little New England village by the sea.

When I used to visit Canada on business
the only way anyone knew I was from
America or an Armenian was from my
American cigarette smoke which is
universally hated worldwide. I did not
realize how bad it smelled until after I
quit smoking. Canadians also tell me
that American food tastes bad too. Oh
well.

When I visited places on business in the
United States the only way people knew
I was from New York was from my dark
suit selection. Otherwise the What is
He line never came up. And I have been
in roadhouse bars in the middle of
nowhere in Georgia buying bourbon for
everyone and no one was saying What is
He? This was especially true when you

were telling New York jokes in places
like Texas where the big line was You
Love NY then take I84 East.

And that is how you create your identity
in response to your environment or
your fears.

Chapter 4

So what does it mean to be Armenian? Even though I do not speak the language or eat the food frequently or attend a church it is the shared history which binds me to my people and defines me as Armenian.

When I asked for submissions from Armenians on their thoughts on their identities in their own words some people sent CVs rather than a short essay which is great because that really goes to the point of who we are, or rather, What is He? To which I say Inch' e na? Shant baner. Many things.

"Hello , it's my pleasure ,

My name is Edna Zargarian , I was born
in and grew up in Jolfa , Esfahan in a
family who proudly keep and love
Armenian culture, language and
heritage"

"By training, a historian specializing in
modern Armenian history, Aram Arkun
is Executive Director of the Tekeyan
Cultural Association of the US and
Canada and Assistant Editor of the
Armenian Mirror-Spectator (formerly
director of the Krikor and Clara Zohrab
Information Center of the Eastern
Diocese of the Armenian Church of

America; formerly editor of Ararat quarterly). "

"Nikit Ariazn-Argishti (Lalik) Mirzayan was born on June 29, 1953 in New Julfa. He received his primary education in the "Shah Abbas" of Armenian N. Juba, "Bustan" (Margarit Sarvaryan) and "Kushesh Davtyan" Teheran, then in "Hashim Sanah" Secondary School in Isfahan. He graduated from Metallurgical Engineering at Tehran's Sharif (formerly Ariameh) Technological University in 1978.

He has national, cultural and social activities, has been a member of NJJA's

Representative and Parliamentary meetings and relevant bodies. He was one of the founding members of the National Iranian-Armenian Cultural and Cultural Union (NMMC, 1981). Founded by "Armen" Chess Club in Njjuba 2001, which is the first private club in Iran.

Has collaborated with Armenian and Persian press in Iran, has a number of historical, philological, ethnographic, journalistic and translation articles. His following works have been published:

"The thirteenth" by Gagik Hakobyan, Armenia, ed. Honey. 1990...

"The thirteenth" by Gagik Hakobyan, Armenia, ed. Honey. 1990

"Armenian Chess Team", gathered and translated, 1998

"Intuition in the process of scientific work", prof. AA Nalchajyan, Armenia, Education. Honey. 2007

"My Honorable 60 Games", Babie Fischer, Armenia, Tarkhaberd. 2008

Avetik M., a founder of the Family of Amirian or Amirkhanians (1736-1921) Compiled and studied by Amirian, Nikit Mirzayan, Njjha, 2012

"Tables from New Julfa Ashugh" (handwritten scrapbook in 1876), worked with Nikit Mirzayan, Njjha, 2017

"Map of salvation", film producer, producer Manvel Saribekyan, script Anna Sargsyan, director Aram Shahbazyan, Tramp. Honey. 2017""

"So it's different for different Armenians
but there are many many areas of
commonalities

I happen to come from a very traditional
family, meaning the villages of my
forefathers kept many ancient
Armenian traditions, ceremonies,
rituals, etc.

Our clan's dances, for instance, didn't
survive for instance but the group LHS
of Armenians that kept the main bulk of
ancient Armenian dance and song forms

are from Sassoon, Mush, also Karin
states.

My cluster group has kept alive many of
the ancient rituals surrounded the
"toner" or "doner" (holidays)

I like to think of the Armenian identity
as that rich spiritual-cultural tradition
that Armenians have maintained For me
the tough part of defining what it is to
be Armenian is trying to capture in
words spiritual phenomena: how a
mother loving and wise eminence (e.g.
touch, song, words...) guide the health
and excellence of the mind of a baby, a
child...illennia (and some have lost some
of it only relatively recently), that very

richness that allowed the Armenian civilization thrive for centuries and centuries. Our culture has something unique in it that let's us grow up wanting to seek the Truth doing the best work possible in any venture (this I think is an essential real-Armenian characteristic) , thus the disproportionately high number of Armenian American inventors who have propelled the development of the US, for instance.

How natural abundant virtues bake the soul of a young Armenian" - - Artin Parsanian

"Hi,dear Michael. I'm Armen Malumyan.
I'm Armenian. I was born in 1969 in St.
Petersburg (Russia) in a family of
artists. I have been living in Armenia
(Yerevan City) for more than forty
years. I'm a professional physicist and
have graduated from Yerevan State
University with honors

in 1991. I worked at school as a teacher
of mathematics. I've been occupied with
the art of glyptics for more than twenty
- five years. I'm a cameo carver. I've
learned this art from my father who was
a professional artist.

I work with seashell, mother - of - pearl

and bone. I'm a folk master of the

Republic of Armenia. I take an active

part in art exhibitions, organized by the

Artists' Union of Armenia. I've

participated in eight exhibitions up to

now. In 2017 I founded " Cameo Carvers

& Friends Art Gallery " on Facebook in

which united carvers from different

countries of the world. You can see

some of my works both in that gallery

and on my personal page called Cameos

by Armen Malumyan.

.   The best regards"

"I am so proud to be an Armenian. Growing up as a child I took everything for granted no matter how much or how little I had. Never ever realizing what my parents or grandparents went through with the genocide of 1915 because they never talked about it. How fortunate I am to be from such strong intelligent people. They came to America and worked hard, became businessmen, professionals and educators and so much more. Who wouldn't be proud to be an Armenian! "
-- Lucille Agababian

"I was born in New York City and am the son of Armenian immigrants who came to the United States and survived the Armenian Genocide of 1915. My mother was a child of five years old when she arrived with her mother preceded by her father. In my dad's case, he was the first in his family who went through the Ellis Island experience. He was a young man, approximately fourteen years old, and was the prototype of a "classic immigrant" arriving 100 years ago.

Furthermore, he told me when he saw the Statue of Liberty for the first time he felt "secure and free." His family was his widowed mother and siblings who followed him on different ships. By his correspondences, he advised and supported their arrivals.

When I was a young man, I remember a large photo which I had

seen of my paternal grandfather. His
name was "Garabed Kulhanjian." It was
then I realized after asking my
grandmother what happened to him
that he along with other members of my
paternal and maternal families were
victims of the Armenian Genocide in
1915. The photo captivated me as I
grew older when others would say there
was a likeness of it to my father as well
as me.

 So explaining the question of: "Who I
Am?" Growing up in the United States,
my perspective of the connection with
my ancestry and kinship to my
descendants was deep in my feeling
and thinking. I had never felt in my
mind I had to be transformed for
feeling Armenian or being American. My

hope was to always to share my heritage which originated in a distant past unknown to others. As a descendant of immigrants, I did not think I had to adopt to a new country, as they did, but I had to become a resourceful citizen and share the American dream they cherished so much. Immigrants became Americans by assimilation and acculturation and their children were born Americans by circumstances unlike those immigrants who immigrated to other nations. "   by
– Gary A. Kulhanjian

"American born with ancestry from Armenia and Sicily can be interesting as I am able to standback and observe each group of people. My first

92

recollection of being Armenian was attending the Armenian Church Sunday school before I started public school. This church was where my grandparents and later my parents were married in and attended. The Armenians are one of the few Christian groups who were proselytized by two apostles of Jesus who were Thaddeus and Bartholomew. The Armenian Church was founded by St. Gregory, the Illuminator, and by 301 AD it was the first state religion in the world.

Then my dear mother gave me a Golden Book, so popular for children in the early 1950s about Noah's Ark from the Bible that my grandchildren still have to this day. I asked my mom how to say the name of that mountain—

"Ararat" and she told me and added that this mountain where Noah landed on was in the historic lands of Armenia from where my family came. I was so happy to hear this and embraced my mom's words from then on, feeling that my heritage was inspiring. When other children asked me what I was, I told them Armenian Christian from the land of Noah which was controlled by Turkey after World War I and the Armenian Genocide of 1915. I never denied that I was half Sicilian also.

With my church group in 1968, I visited Israel, Lebanon, Italy, and traveled to Armenia   which was controlled by the Soviet Russia. We couldn't visit the western side of Armenia since Soviet Russia and Turkey were hostile with each other. Although hiking some through the rugged land it was like nothing I had ever seen before, the terrain was beautiful with snow   peaked Mount Ararat which could be seen in the distance. The aromatic foods, musical notes from medieval instruments, and some of the spoken words were familiar to me from my upbringing. When I visited the first Cathedral, I caught myself thinking these beautiful sharagans (hymns) floating out of the open window of the first church in Armenia on this summer Sunday, were the very same I sang in the church choir weekly far away in the United States.

To feel Armenian or any other nationality you might be, I think you have to be exposed to its culture, educated some in its history and accomplishments. If you speak to some of your descendants who wish to continue their heritage, you will become enlightened and feel pride.

 Let other people you come in contact with know from where you came and they in turn, so the world will be a better place for all of us to live in. "   by- Dolores (nee Baglieri) Kulhanjian

"To me, being of Armenian descent means, being part of a people and culture that extends back thousands and thousands of years. Connected to a rich culture made up of artists, musicians, laborers, sewers, rug makers,

96

farmers, architects, intellectuals, religious leaders and so forth. An ethnic group from which an alphabet and language of its own was birthed.   Armenians were one of the first believers in Christ, forming the world's first Christian nation, and clinging on to their belief for centuries when repeatedly threatened. It means having a lineage of fortitude to overcome tragedy, multiple attempted conquests, and Genocide. It demonstrates the strength of the collective community and individual ability of a people to not only overcome but to flourish. To me it means knowing and recognizing that I am the living testament of my great and great-great-grandfathers who were innocently killed; and to my grandparents who came to America to start their lives over in a "new world". I am part of their story, and they live within me." – Gregory Kulhanjian

I would like to thank everyone for participating in this endeavor.

End

Arkun, Aram, Jan Balakian: Praising American Playwrights, The Armenian Mirror Spectator, June 10, 2010

Aslanian, David Sebough, From the Indian Ocean to the Mediterranean the Global Trade Networks of Armenian Merchants from New Julfa, University of California Press, 2014

Balakian, Krikor, The Ruins of Ani: A Journey to Armenia's Medieval Capital and Its Legacy, trans. Aram Arkun and Peter Balakian, Rutgers University Press.

Balakian, Peter, Black Dog of Fate: A Memoir, Basic Books, 2009.

Baliozian, Ara, Portait of a Genius and Other Essays A/G Press, 1980.

Beshlian, Hagop A, A Shirt for the Brave, Introduction by Gary A. Kulhanjian, Gomidas Institute, 2017

Bournoutian, George A., A History of the Armenian People: Pre History to 1500 AD; A History of the Armenian People: 1500 AD to the Present, Mazda Publishers, 1994, 1995.

Boyajian, Michael, The History of the Armenian Speaking People, Jera Studios Publishing, 2018.

Cash, Adam, Psychology for Dummies, For Dummies, 2013

Chahin, M., The Kingdom of Armenia, Dorset Press, 1987

Heshmat, Shahram, Psychology Today, December 8, 2014

Hovannisian, Richard G., editor, The Armenian People from Ancient to Modern Times, St. Martin's Press 2004.

James, Paul, Despite the Terrors of Typologies: The Importance of Difference and Identity, Intervention Journal of Postcolonial Studies, 2015

Kulhanjian, Gary A., An Abstract of the Historical and Sociological Aspects of Armenian Immigration to the United States: 1890 to 1930, A and E Research Associates, 1975.

Leary, MR and Tagney, JP, Handbook of
Self and Identity, Guilford Press, 2003

Manandyan, Hakob., Tigranes II and
Rome, trans. George A. Bournutian,
Mazda Publishers 2007

Merryl, Wyn, Davies and Piero,
Introducing Anthropology, Icon Books,
2002

Morgenthau, Henry, Ambassador
Morgenthau's Story: A Personal Acount
of the Armenian Genocide, Doubleday,
Page and Co., 1918

Moses of Chorene, History of Arenai, trans BP Pratten, Dalesossion Publishing 2017.

Payaslian, Simon, The History of Armenia, Palgrave MacMillan, 2007

Redgate, AE, The Armenians, Blackwell Publishers, 1998.

Seth, Mesrob Jacob, History of the Armenians in India from the Earliest Times to the Present Day, Forgotten Books, 2017

Soulhaian, Rita, The Survivor: Biography
of Aram Andonian, Gomidas Institute,
2013.

YouTube: CivilNet: Topic: Armenian
Identity

June 3, 2014

October 19, 2014

April 27, 2017

September, 22 2017

May 28, 2018

About the Author

Michael Boyajian is a retired attorney and a former human rights judge. He has written The History of the Armenian Speaking People and 24 other books. He lives in the Hudson Valley with his wife Jeri Wagner and their three cats where they enjoy their Cicero garden and library.